H

BEGINNER'S TO INTERMEDIATE HOW TO HACK GUIDE TO COMPUTER HACKING, PENETRATION TESTING AND BASIC SECURITY

TABLE OF CONTENTS

INTRODUCTION

The very fact that you are reading my book is an indicator that you are interested in learning the fine art of hacking. You could also be concerned with the safety and security of your home or office computer system or network -- and who isn't, these days?

Computer hacking is the act of "breaking" into a computer system or network by modifying hardware or software to do things that the manufacturer definitely did not intend them to do. Hacking used to be an activity done purely for fun and the spirit of adventure: an activity that people got into, individually or as a collective, just to see if they could succeed.

Nowadays, however, when people think of hacking they think of hijacking hardware or software -- of getting these things to perform all kinds of malicious actions. Every week we read about another major company or financial institution that has been hacked into, resulting in the theft of customer data, or massive amounts of money, or information held by financial insiders, or even trade secrets. Now more than ever, it's vitally important that you keep both your computer and your Internet connection safe and secure so that you don't become the next victim.

You've heard of unethical hackers -- what about the ethical hackers? Ethical hackers, sometimes referred to as the "white hats", are the hackers who work at keeping individual users and companies safe. Indeed, some of the world's biggest hackers have gone on to provide the world with technology that is useful and constructive -- and perhaps one of the best-known of them all was the late Steve Jobs, co-founder of the mighty Apple company. He started out as a hacker, and went on to provide us with cutting edge technology and innovative hardware.

Unethical or malicious hackers, sometimes referred to as the "black hats", can face prison time and heavy fines if caught. And a cracker, a person who breaks through security codes to steal personal information or destroy an information system, can face prison sentences of up to 20 years. Let that be a lesson to anyone who is considering becoming a cracker or an unethical hacker.

In my book, I am going to give you an overview of hacking and penetration testing. I am going to show you how it's done, and then I'm going to tell you how to keep your systems secure so that you can't be hacked!

DISCLAIMER

Breaking into a computer or Internet system with malicious intent is a criminal offense. I have written this book purely for informational purposes. I will not be held responsible for any misuse of this information or any illegal activities that arise from it.

CHAPTER 1

WHAT IS HACKING?

Machines and networks made of machines and the instructions that make them go -- these things are not without their weaknesses -- and the same is true whether we're talking about a production line, an intranet that exists within one division of a multinational company, or the worldwide conglomeration of computers, computer networks, and software that we call the Internet.

You can put locks on the doors of a factory to protect the machines and the flow of the process. You can shut down the modems and take out the cables that connect the computers in the intranet to each other and only to each other. You can't do that with the Internet -- and that's the reason why we need to learn about cybersecurity. Also known as computer security or IT security, cybersecurity encompasses everything to do with the protection of information systems.

Cybersecurity seeks to prevent the theft of information held in these systems; it also seeks to protect these systems themselves from damage or intentional misuse.

In the world of cybersecurity, the person who can find a vulnerability or weakness in a system, or who can get into that vulnerability and exploit it, is called a hacker. There are still those who think that hacking is as simple and as easy as getting into someone's Facebook or Twitter account without their knowledge or consent. Or they think that the be-all and end-all of hacking is in defacing a website to show silly or obscene or provocative messages. But these things are small beer in the grand scheme of the world of hackers.

Before you learn how to become a hacker, you should learn about the different types of hackers, and become familiar with their similarities and differences.

SCRIPT KIDDIE

These hackers use programs, tools, and scripts created by other hackers, instead of creating their own. They don't tend to know how systems work, but will happily use already available tools to hack.

WHITE HAT HACKER

Otherwise known as ethical hackers. White Hat Hackers are the good guys, and they do what they do in order to keep the rest of us safe. By locating flaws in information systems and doing their best to fix them, they improve cybersecurity as a whole. They tend to work for large organizations.

BLACK HAT HACKER

These are the unethical hackers who hack for malicious purposes. They steal customer data or money, infect a system with malware, or make information systems do things that they're not supposed to do.

GREY HAT HACKER

These hackers are on the fence, so to speak. They don't hack for malicious purposes but will still break into an information system just to show that they have the chops to do it, or just to show that there are flaws in that system. If they do work with a company, they might present a solution to the flaws that they found only AFTER they have hacked into that company's information system.

HACKTIVISTS

The word "hacktivist" is a portmanteau of the words "hacker" and "activist". They break into information systems for the sake of protesting against injustice and for the sake of working towards social justice -- or sometimes just to perform some wild publicity stunts. Hacktivists have been appearing more and more often in the headlines as of late, with the most famous of them being Anonymous.

HOW TO BECOME A HACKER

The road to becoming a good hacker is long and complicated, and one of the first things to learn before taking the first step on that road is the proper programming language to use. Every website and system is built using one or more computer languages, and in order to hack these sites or systems successfully, you must first understand those languages. The following are the languages that you'll need to understand for each particular purpose.

WEB HACKING

If you want to be able to hack websites you'll need to read, code, and understand the following computer languages, all of which play vital parts in the display and functioning of different web-based content.

- HTML -- standing for Hypertext Markup Language, this is the standard markup language that is used in creating and modifying web pages.
- CSS -- standing for Cascading Style Sheets, this is a style sheet language that is used to define the physical appearance / presentation of a document that has been written in a markup language. As such, it is used hand-in-hand with HTML.
- JavaScript -- used in both online and offline forms, it is used to create, support, and display everything from web pages to PDFs.
- PHP -- a server-side scripting language used mostly for designing web pages, but it is now also used to create other kinds of computer programs.
- SQL -- standing for Structured Query Language, this is used to manage information that is coded into a database, or that is in the form of a data stream.

WRITING EXPLOITS

In addition, a hacker with knowledge of the computer languages Ruby and Python will have a huge advantage, as they are both used in writing exploits.

But what is an exploit? An exploit, in the context of cybersecurity, takes advantage of a known or a discovered bug or vulnerability in an information system. It could take the form of a piece of software, an amount of data, or even a sequence of commands. These allow a hacker to get further into an information system than might have been originally intended.

• Ruby -- a relatively programmer-friendly language that's designed to be easy to learn, but it can yield massively complex results. This object-oriented programming language can and has been used in writing exploits, as it has a great deal of flexibility in its syntax and variables. The Metasploit framework, which we will discuss further on in this book, is built on Ruby.

• Python -- another widely-used programming language that supports the creation of programs that are easy to read, no matter the size of the program or the intended functions. It is the core language for creating hacking tools and writing exploits.

REVERSE ENGINEERING

There are many ways of looking into a piece of software in order to learn how it's built and how it works -- and in reverse engineering, the hacker works backwards from the published product. The hacker looks at the software and what it does, and deduces the code, the functionalities, and the process flow that might produce the observed results. This might be considered by some to be a low-level form of coding, though it can actually yield very advanced results, especially in cases where the source code/s can no longer be obtained, or where the source code is not easy to find or modify.

Anyone who learns how to reverse-engineer code will be able to break down, understand, and modify many different kinds of programs, as well as many different forms of hardware. A working knowledge of assembly languages will come in handy. There are many different assembly languages, each specific to the architecture of a particular computer system.

These are just a few of the languages that you need to learn in order to become a hacker. Now we are going to look at a way to find most every vulnerability and exploit there is to find.

At the end of the book, you can find a list of resources where you'll find more information on the languages and procedures described here.

FINDING EXPLOITS AND VULNERABILITIES

While there are many tools that can be used in order to investigate the various vulnerabilities of information systems, in this book we will zero in on the SecurityFocus database.

It's a rare thing indeed to find the exploits that you need during your first run at hacking into an information system. Don't rely on blind luck: use your head and use the tools that are already available to you.

First: do some research. What will work on your target, and what won't? Take a look at the operating system that the target is using, and once you've pinpointed that, then it will be easier to look for open ports and exploitable servers. From there, you can determine the best way to compromise the target without detection and that is not always going to be an obvious solution.

You will likely want to put in a little work in order to find the right vulnerabilities to exploit in your target information system -- and then to find the corresponding tools that can work on those vulnerabilities. This tutorial is all about finding those vulnerabilities and exploits.

Step 1

Using a browser that you can trust, head to the URL www.securityfocus.com. The database contains quite a few tools that you can use to search for vulnerabilities. You can run searches in a number of ways including the Common Vulnerability and Exploit number, also known as the CVE number. This number is assigned by the MITRE Corporation, a non-profit organization funded by a section of the US Homeland Security department.

Step 2

The CVE database is full of vulnerabilities. Most every vulnerability that has been found is included here, including those vulnerabilities that the software publishers would prefer to keep hidden. Let's take Adobe for an example. The last few years have not been kind to Adobe thanks to software that has been poorly designed, resulting in releases that are absolutely jam-packed with vulnerabilities. Just about every single computer has Adobe Reader and/or Adobe Flash installed, which leaves that computer and any networks it might be connected to open to an attack. For this section, we are going to focus on Adobe Flash Player.

Step 3

In SecurityFocus, click on the Vendors tab and select Flash Player from the menu. Click on Submit and you will be presented with a list of vulnerabilities that exist in Adobe Flash Player. Information on each vulnerability exists on that list, as do different ways of exploiting those vulnerabilities. For example, one of these vulnerabilities will allow you to install a rootkit or listener on any system running Flash Player. These programs will give you access to that system as though you were an actual registered user on that system.

Step 4

Having found the vulnerabilities in your targeted information system, the next step to take involves finding the actual exploits that might be relevant to your objectives. The remote code execution vulnerabilities are likely to be present on virtually every computer system. A vulnerability is a weakness in the system that can be exploited, but that doesn't mean that someone has managed to get in and perform the actual exploit.

While you're going to need a few advanced skills in programming in order to develop your own exploits, it's easy as long you're talented.

So, to find an exploit for the vulnerability, click the Exploit tab in the SecurityFocus window. In the results you'll see the exploits that have already been developed for the particular vulnerability you chose. If the vulnerability is brand-new, there will be no exploits. Develop your skills in programming using the languages that were listed in the previous sections, and you can use those skills to be the first person to come up with an exploit for a new vulnerability.

This chapter covered how to find vulnerabilities and how to find the exploits for those vulnerabilities. With this information you can go on to use the exploits to get into a system through a vulnerability.

CHAPTER 2

WHAT IS PENETRATION TESTING?

Before we talk about penetration testing, we need to take a serious look at the differences between a hacker, an ethical hacker, and a penetration tester.

- A hacker is a person or a group of people who hack into an information system or computer network without the actual users' permission -- and they usually perform that action for malicious purposes, such as stealing the data that's being held in that system.

- An ethical hacker is a professional hacker who is hired to look at security for a company or organization's information system. It is the ethical hacker's task to test that information system for vulnerabilities. If they are directly contracted to work with a company or an organization, it might also fall to them to continue monitoring that company or organization's information systems for the purpose of ongoing optimization and protection.

- A penetration tester is a professional whose work goes beyond that of an ethical hacker. Companies and organizations employ penetration testers to check for vulnerabilities, investigating those systems from the point of view of a hacker who is trying to gain unauthorized access. Penetration testers might be called upon to provide a full analysis of these companies' information systems and cybersecurity. It is the job of the penetration tester to find vulnerabilities -- anything from poor configuration of hardware or software, or operational weaknesses.

WHAT IS A PENETRATION TEST?

A penetration test, otherwise known as a "pen test", is the practice of performing an attack on an information system in exactly the same way as a hacker would, but without causing any actual damage to that system. Penetration testing requires the permission of the system owner, and should not proceed without that permission. If you don't get the permission in writing, in the form of a contract, you are nothing more than a hacker. That is the fundamental difference between hacking and penetration testing.

To give you a bit of background on penetration testing, we first need to look at what this testing does, and what a penetration tester is looking for. Penetration testers look for vulnerabilities, which are holes in the security of a system. These holes are what allow hackers to access the system. They can be anything: they can be as simple as a weak password, or they can be as complex as SQL injection vulnerabilities or buffer overflows.

Security researchers are the people who find vulnerabilities and look for ways to break them. To take advantage of that vulnerability and use it as an entry point into a system, you'll need something called an exploit. This is a small piece of very specialized software -- so specialized, in fact, that it only has one purpose: to get in through a specific vulnerability and give the hacker access to the system in which that vulnerability exists. Many exploits deliver a payload -- that is, a program or a sequence of programs -- that give the hacker access to, and sometimes control of, the entire system.

A payload is normally attached to the exploit and is delivered by the exploit. Metasploit is a project that contains the world's largest public database of all exploits that are quality-assured. The most popular payload in Metasploit is called Meterpreter -- and this payload allows you do a variety of things to a target system. For example, using Meterpreter, you can make your targeted information system download and upload files, or you can make it take screenshots, or you can make it collect passwords and password hashes. The right code, delivered via Meterpreter, can even allow you to take control of your targeted information system, or switch on a webcam attached to the system and use it for spying purposes.

How to Get Started with Penetration Testing

The first step in penetration testing is knowing exactly what it is you are looking for. And then comes practice: don't rely on others' code to automate your penetration testing! Do it yourself, one line of code at a time if it comes to it -- this gives you the practice you'll need and the time you'll want in order to keep enhancing your penetration testing skills.

Consider starting small -- but don't think of it as playing for small change. Web apps and web-reliant programs are among the most common targets for hackers, and that's because of the lucky convergence of several factors. One, web apps and the like tend to be relatively smaller in terms of the amount of code involved, which means you don't have to put so much time into analyzing for possible vulnerabilities.

Two, web apps are so common! They're found on so many platforms -- desktop and laptop computers, tablets, smartphones, and many other devices. You can even practice on your own units and build up the confidence you'll need to perform penetration testing on other platforms.

Three, web apps tend to have relatively simple vulnerabilities, and these can be used to obtain access to data, up to and including personal information. From there, it's easy to find personal information or the other objectives of the penetration test.

And one more thing about performing penetration tests on web apps: while it's a nearly universal truth that firewalls and security controls are now part and parcel for any information system, they are still vulnerable to attacks that target and exploit specific web apps. This is the critical reason why every person and organization must ensure that their web apps are protected from common attacks.

SQL Injection

When you carry out an SQL injection attack on a targeted information system as part of penetration testing, you are inserting or injecting an SQL query into the system by using the data that comes directly from a client. If successful, an SQL injection exploit can read or record sensitive data, make changes to the system by inserting new data, update or delete data, carry out admin-only operations on the database, and recover file contents. In some cases, it may even be able to send commands to the target operating system.

THE 5 PHASES OF PENETRATION TESTING

Reconnaissance

This is the longest part of the testing and can take weeks or even months. Hackers use a number of ways to find information about their targeted system and its properties and operations. These methods include searching the Internet, domain name management, social engineering, etc.

There is no defense against the activities in the first phase. Information can find its way onto the Internet in many different ways, even down to employees being tricked into revealing information. This means that it's up to the organization to make sure their systems -- and people -- are secure.

Scanning

Once you have gained sufficient information to understand how a business operates and what information could be valuable to you, your next job is to scan the internal networks and the perimeter of that business. You'll be looking for weaknesses such as open services and ports, apps that can be targeted (including the operating system), unprotected or vulnerable data in transit, and quite possibly even the makes and model numbers of the LAN and WAN equipment.

Be aware that perimeter and internal device scans can sometimes be detected by IDS (Intrusion Detection) or IPS (Prevention) services, but this isn't always the case. If you wanted to avoid these sorts of scans on your systems you would need to close all the ports and services that you don't use. You'll also need to change the settings on your systems so that critical devices or those that hold and process sensitive information can only respond to a device that has been approved.

Gaining Access

This is the point of any modern-day attack. The objectives of such an attack can fall into two broad categories: obtain valuable information, or use the targeted system or network as a jump-off point for an attack against a different target. Either way, the attacker has to be able to access at least one network device.

It is down to the system administrator and security managers to ensure that servers and end-user devices are protected against any and all forms of unauthorized access. This will often include the denial of admin privileges to unauthenticated users, as well as keeping a close eye on the accesses that local admin and the domain might have to the servers.

Highly sensitive information and keys need to be encrypted. Even if you have a weak security system, encryption is often a good defense against attackers, although it shouldn't be the only protective system in place.

Maintaining Access

Once they have gained access, a hacker has to stay in the system long enough to carry out their actual objectives, as mentioned above. Just because the hacker -- or the penetration tester -- has already gotten through the implemented security measures successfully doesn't mean their work is done, as it is in this phase that the risk of actual detection by the information system's gatekeepers or administrators is highest.

As well as using IPS and IDS devices to detect an intruder, you can also use them to monitor outgoing information. For example:

- Detect files that are being transferred to an external site, and prevent those transfers from being completed

- Prevent the initiation of a prolonged or unauthorized connection between your servers and systems or networks that are out of your control

- Monitor and prevent uplinks to strange ports

- Monitor and terminate sessions that are unusually long or carried out frequently, and keep track of the amount of content that is being transferred

Covering Tracks

Once the hacker has completed all of the actions that are to be deployed against the targeted information system, they must then hide their tracks -- and, more importantly, conceal any controls that they may have left in place in order to facilitate future actions, or to continue in monitoring the target.

This is where the security manager comes in: it's up to this person to make sure that the information system is clear of any unauthorized intrusions, and remains clear as such. A security manager can deny their business users admin privileges, and stop them from accessing desktops except at designated hours. A security manager might also limit the number of users who can get into the system at any given time.

It is the overriding responsibility of the security manager and of the system administrators to have absolute and complete knowledge of the ins and outs of their information systems -- and they have to keep in mind that the hacker, or the penetration tester, will probably know just as much about those same information systems as they do. Perhaps even more.

As a penetration tester, you'll need to be a top-level hacker. You'll have to know your way around the information system you're testing, and not only that -- you'll have to get into and around different networks. You'll need to be able to think like a hacker to know exactly what they're going to do. Otherwise, you don't stand a chance of stopping them.

CHAPTER 3

BASIC SECURITY

Every time you switch on your computer and access the Internet, you make yourself vulnerable to catching a virus. And it's nothing as ordinary as a virus that makes you sneeze or hack up a lung, either. We are talking about the kinds of viruses that used to be nothing more than annoying chain letters or badly-edited images -- but now we have become painfully aware of how these viruses can completely and irretrievably shut down your PC or mobile device. And it gets worse -- you might very well transmit that virus to other PCs or devices on the networks that you use, before you lose the infected item.

Worse still is the possibility of the virus turning your computer into a portal. In other words, an access point that allows the original attackers -- or, worse, new ones -- to conduct all manner of vicious and sinister activities. We're talking about anything from the ability to hack other websites, a Denial of Service attack, or even the theft of personal and confidential data for the purposes of committing cybercrime or fraud.

So what kind of loss could you be looking at when your system gets attacked by a virus? For home-based PC users, they might feel irritation but also a fleeting sense of having dodged a bullet -- after all, for them, all they have to do is lose a day or two in getting and installing a new operating system in the aftermath of a virus attack. The truth is, one virus attack against one home-based PC user is a very small intrusion.

But take a look at the situation from the point of view of a company, whether it's a small one or a large one, and the difference becomes clear. Just one virus attack against that company's PCs and information systems means quite a loss -- and the effects of that loss can be disproportionately large compared to the size of the company that got attacked. It could be more difficult for a small company to recover from that attack.

Let's look at an example from 2005 -- and before you think that was a long time ago, think of it in terms of the consequences, which are still being felt today.

In 2005, Sony BMG (at that time a record distribution company, among other things) was discovered to have been including potentially harmful copy-protection software on millions of audio CDs. When an audio CD from Sony BMG was loaded onto a PC, it would play the encoded music, but it would also install software which would modify the operating system of that PC to prevent the copying of the music from that CD. Nowadays we would consider that to be an application of the ideas behind digital rights management as well as a primitive form of copy protection -- but what really set the scandal off was the fact that the software created vulnerabilities in the PCs that they were installed in, making those units vulnerable to malware.

What's more, at least one of the pieces of software that Sony BMG was underhandedly distributing using its audio CDs would actually send data on an affected user's listening habits back to Sony BMG. These programs also modified the affected PCs' operating systems to hide their existence from the PC's actual user, meaning they were actually mass-distributed rootkits.

As a result of this scandal, suits were filed against Sony BMG in various parts of the United States, and countries such as Italy called for investigations into allegations that Sony BMG had actually committed cybercrime against its consumers. Sony BMG went defunct in 2008 after another series of scandals, but it was the rootkit that was the first major herald of its closure.

Since then, more and more tech leaders and consumers have campaigned for and against copy protection, as well as for or against digital rights management -- and many of these leaders and consumers are also on the alert for rootkits and the possibility of exploits coming from the programs and applications that they use.

On the other hand, it was as a result of this scandal that people all over the world became aware of the existence of these types of often-malicious software. Now it's easier to understand that a rootkit is a single software application, or a collection of such applications, that are designed to give a user -- usually an unauthorized user -- access to a computer or to parts of its installed software that normally would not be accessed. At the same time, a rootkit conceals itself from the actual authorized user of that computer -- or, alternatively, conceals other applications from the authorized user.

HOW TO PROTECT YOURSELF FROM TROJANS OR A VIRUS

These days, almost everybody has access to the Internet, and almost anyone can learn how to build a website. However, there are some web developers who hurry to create websites, with the result that they can skim over the important part of looking through their code for bugs. Computers can easily end up infected with a virus when people are not careful about security. A virus can: cause a computer to crash; make files behave in a strange manner; make odd messages appear; or load unrequested web pages. The worst-case scenario is that a virus that gets through can destroy not just an end-user's operating system, but go on to infect other computers.

Computer viruses are actually very subtle. They tend to be installed onto the system only when a file, program, or email attachment that contains the virus is opened or executed. From there, the virus will then reproduce itself, similar to the biological viruses that we get. It does this by attaching a copy of itself to another program that is on the hard drive. Where it goes from there and what else it does other than reproduce, depends entirely on the creator of the virus.

Some viruses are just silly jokes that pop up messages: you could get a "Merry Christmas" message, or an image that makes it appear like the image displayed on your monitor is melting down. Many, however, are malicious, and upon execution will begin to systematically destroy the computer system. A virus can either bring down the files straight away, or cause the system to self-destruct on a given date that has been specified in the virus, similar to the very public Michelangelo virus that was set to erase important data from systems on March 6.

Similar to a virus, a Trojan horse program affects a computer system, but unlike a virus it does not reproduce and send copies of itself outward. Trojan horses disguise themselves as benign and useful software, and that's how they lure users to download them voluntarily. They are modified to look like useful software -- but once they are downloaded and then executed, they're freed to wreak havoc upon your computer and/or your operating system. Trojan horses might cause odd messages to pop up on the screen or, as in the case of a modified version of the popular PKZip utility from PKWare, it could erase the entire hard drive.

A virus or Trojan requires that the program, website, or utility that it's attached to be launched in order to activate. This is part of the reason why many viruses and Trojans spread by means of appearing as attachments to emails -- the moment people open these emails to read, not knowing they are actually hoaxes, the virus or the Trojan executes. But if the attachment isn't opened or the email isn't read, the virus or the Trojan is rendered harmless.

The problem lies in the fact that many people do not know what they are looking for, and end up unwittingly launching the program or the Trojan. By the time they notice that something's gone wrong with their systems, it's too late because the damage has already been done.

PROTECTING YOURSELF

There is a set of basic rules that all computer users should follow to stop viruses in their tracks, and these rules are true for home-based PC users and business PC users alike.

The most obvious piece of advice is to never open any email attachment unless you are 100% certain you know whom it is from and why it has been sent to you. If you avoid opening junk email or email from people that you don't recognize, then you can't download a virus; it's as simple as that. One of the best ways to detect if an email has a virus is to use an anti-virus program. I will talk a little more about that in the next section.

A related piece of advice is to make use of the Spam folders that are included in many web-based email utilities. If you receive an email and you neither recognize it nor signed up for it, you can send it straight to the Spam folder and not have to worry about accidentally opening it up, therefore protecting you from whatever malicious attachments might lie within.

Do a little research on the Internet before going to a newly-opened website, or downloading a new web app -- read the reviews and study the possible glitches or vulnerabilities before committing to the download.

If you do download software from the Internet, run the file or files through an anti-virus program before executing them. Sure, it adds one more step to the download and installation, but it's a few seconds spent on keeping your computer and operating system safe, and therefore time spent wisely.

Protecting a computer can be time-consuming. If you want to be safe and secure using your computer and the Internet, you'll have to put in the time to make it work -- but trust me, the time that you spend now will potentially save you a lot of frustration and heartache later on, not to mention the money and the time that it will take to rebuild your system.

Viruses are not the only things you have to be wary of. There are other programs that have been written to cripple a system or to make use of your computer in an unauthorized way: these other types of malware include, but are not limited to, worms, logic bombs, and rootkits (as detailed above).

Next, we are going to look at ways in which you can protect yourself with the use of basic security measures.

TOP 10 SECURITY PRACTICES EVERYONE SHOULD BE FOLLOWING

I can't possibly cover every single security measure out there, but in my opinion these are the most important things to do. These are the best ways to maintain computer security while on the Internet.

Use Anti-Virus Software

This should be chalked up to nothing more than common sense, but you'd be surprised at the number of people who simply don't have any anti-virus software, much less any malware detectors, installed on their computers. While the Windows operating system does contain its own software solutions, these are by no means perfect, and you really shouldn't rely on it alone to protect you and your system. If you do, you are putting yourself at risk for an attack.

Many people say that they are careful and that they don't need to use anti-virus software. This is a foolish notion, as these same people might well be surprised at exactly what can infect a computer. Something small like a plugin on the browser for Adobe Flash could very well be infected by a zero-day vulnerability. You wouldn't realize because it's a name you trust and, after all, it's only a plugin, right? And while your browser may be updated fairly regularly, there will always be that time when a new vulnerability appears before the browser is updated to patch it.

Anti-virus software is a vital layer of protection in the fight against viruses -- but you must remember to keep your software up to date! New threats appear on a daily basis, and in order to keep up all of your protective measures, you'll have to update your anti-virus software regularly. Most of the software solutions allow you to modify their settings such that they receive their necessary updates regularly and automatically, but you'll still need to check on it from time to time, in order to make sure that the anti-virus software is working entirely as it should.

Leave UAC Enabled

UAC stands for User Account Control. It was first implemented on Windows when Vista was released. At the time, many users were frustrated and thought that it was nothing more than an obnoxious add-on. However, Microsoft has continued to work on it since it was first released, and it is now far less intrusive than it was before. The worst part about it is the extra pop-up window or two that you might run into when setting up a new computer or when installing new software, but once that is complete, it is no longer bothersome.

The idea behind UAC is that it helps to protect your computer against malicious software, stopping it from being able to modify your system without your permission. Like the anti-virus software, it is a vital layer of protection.

Enable Your Firewall and Configure It Properly

Windows has its own built-in firewall so it shouldn't be necessary to add another one. However, do make sure that whatever firewall implementation you do have is enabled at all times. It is there for a reason -- to stop uninvited incoming connections. This protects both your operating system and your software from malware that can exploit vulnerabilities, particularly those that have not yet been patched, or those that "listen" to your network. In the early days of Windows XP, a worm called Blaster spread like wildfire because of the lack of such a firewall. Firewalls have stopped worms like this from propagating.

It isn't enough to have the firewall enabled, though. It has to be correctly configured in order to work properly. Whenever you get a message asking if you are on a Home, Work or Public Network, make sure you give the correct answer. For example, if you're trying to access the Internet from a coffee shop or using the public-access wi-fi at the mall, don't answer the pop-up by telling it that you're using a Home Network. That simple command can make all of your shared files accessible to everyone on that same network. In this scenario, choosing the Public Network option would stop others from accessing shared resources.

Uninstall Java

This is a name that you trust, right? Unfortunately, most of us are using a version of Java that is both outdated and cannot be completely secured, and that makes it easy to pick up a virus just by opening a web page. It might sound strange, but Java is full of security holes. Every time the developers patch one hole, another two appear in its place. The worst part is that most of us don't even need Java anymore. Java applets are no longer in wide use, and websites that do call for them are now becoming increasingly rare. As such we are leaving ourselves open to attack for no reason.

If you have installed Java on your computer, head to your settings and remove it as soon as you can. You'll be asked to reinstall it if you should need it, so don't worry about removing it. And if you do find yourself reinstalling Java -- say you play a game that requires it to be installed, such as Minecraft -- then make sure you disable the browser plugin to give yourself some protection.

Keep Your Software Fully Up to Date

Every piece of software we use has the potential to be full of security issues, and this is true for practically every category of software. Operating systems such as Windows are notorious for their continuing vulnerability to attacks from malicious programmers. Browsers such as Mozilla Firefox and Google Chrome are less vulnerable than Internet Explorer, but they can be attacked just the same. And entire suites of programs such as the Adobe programs and Microsoft Office share common software features that mean if one program becomes vulnerable to attack, the others might soon follow suit. I could go on and on but I'm sure you get the picture.

Virtually all software providers will release regular updates for their products. One very good reason why you should install these updates and patches as soon as they are released is because of the release notes -- if you have ever read any of these, then you will know that they can often contain information that tells a hacker how to develop an attack against machines that have not been patched!

Users of the Windows operating system should check their settings to make sure that they get regular and automatic updates to the system itself, and the same goes for their installed programs. If this is not always feasible, you should at least check your settings to tell you when new updates are available. All browsers and other major software tend to include the automatic update feature, so make sure you don't disable this -- that way, you will always be running on the very latest patched version of any software.

Browser plugins are one of the most worrisome of all security issues. If you are unsure of whether your plugins are up to date, you can visit the Mozilla Plug-In Check website at https://www.mozilla.org/en-US/plugincheck/. It works on all browsers and will tell you if you need to update your plugins.

Be Wary Of Programs You Install and Run

This might seem obvious, but again you would be surprised at how many people just hit the download button without thinking about what it is that they're actually downloading. And even more people are completely unaware that they might be downloading programs when they think they're just browsing a website. So much of the malware that winds up on our computers comes from careless or thoughtless clicking that downloads programs into the computer.

To avoid these accidental or careless downloads, always be on alert whenever you're online, and always be very careful about what you are doing. Make sure you only download software that you trust. Only get software from official websites. Failing that, look for trusted mirror sites. Never get software from third-party sources.

When you download software, be aware of advert banners that have been cleverly disguised as download links. These will take the user to a completely different site and if you're not careful, you can be conned into downloading software that could very well be malicious.

Also be aware that these "programs" can come in many different forms. For example, a screensaver that is in .SCR format could very easily contain malicious software, so be aware and keep your wits about you at all times.

Don't Download Cracked or Pirate Software

This rule mostly applies to peer-to-peer networks, torrent aggregators, and other obviously shady places. Most of the time it won't be possible for you to check the provenance of the programs that appear on these networks -- you won't know if the computers you're downloading from are themselves virus-free, and you won't know what additional malicious programs might be included in the actual downloads.

If you do insist on downloading from these sites, you are putting yourself right in the line of fire. If you execute files from these places, you are basically putting your trust in the software distributor not to bring any harm to your system.

In many cases, the cracks that will be needed in order to make these pirated programs run correctly are often produced by specific software-cracking teams -- teams that do their very best to stay anonymous. As a result, you will never know whether they have included malware in that crack -- until it's much, much too late.

Of course, downloading actual software is far riskier than downloading a pirated movie file, album, or e-book. This is because the software is actually machine code and that can easily be tampered with. On the other hand, movies, albums, or e-books are just media files -- they will either play or they won't. That said, there are malicious individuals who will disguise malware to look like a video -- so again, the warning to download only from trusted sources holds true here.

Be Very Aware of Phishing and Social Engineering

Most of the major email clients and browsers will do what they can to protect you from a phishing attack, but there is always room for improvement in those measures. A phishing attack is the Internet version of a person who calls you on the phone and pretends to be your bank asking for your bank details or credit card numbers. Banks don't do this sort of thing, either by phone or by email.

Be very aware of online requests for personal information. Make sure that if you do have to give out your card numbers or bank details, you only give them to legitimate websites or individuals. Look for the SSL icon in the address bar of your browser; it might take the form of a closed lock or of a green check mark. The presence of that icon shows that the web page you're currently on is correctly and sufficiently encrypted so as to protect the information that you're about to send.

If you need to access your bank accounts using the online banking facility of your bank, do it through the bank's official website. If you receive an email that purports to be from your bank and that asks for your personal information or account details, do not click on any links in that email! Open a new browser window or tab, and type in the actual address of your bank's official website, and log in to your account using the link from your bank's official website. Doing it any other way might open you up for an attack from phishers, who will attempt to steal your personal details using a an official-looking website.

Phishing might sound like a fairly sneaky way of stealing your personal information -- but it's amateurish compared to theft of personal information by means of social engineering methods. These methods rely on the psychological manipulation of people, forcing them to perform actions that they wouldn't do otherwise, or pushing them to divulge otherwise confidential information.

Some social engineering methods used for hacking and unauthorized entry into otherwise secure networks are almost surprisingly simple: Kevin Mitnick, once a notorious computer hacker and now a cybersecurity consultant, claimed that it was much easier to fool someone into giving out a password to a given computer network or information system, compared to spending hours or days on hacking into that same network or system.

You've actually seen social engineering methods on TV and in the movies, and they aren't even new, as they've even been used by none other than Agent 007 himself, James Bond. The trick is to be aware of them instead of falling for them.

Never Reuse Passwords

Many people reuse their passwords across different accounts and different websites. Using one password to access a number of different sites is dangerous. It only takes one leak -- if your password gets stolen from one website, then it opens up the very real possibility that your data could be stolen from all of the other sites that you use.

Don't think that attackers won't try to login to any number of websites with the same credentials, hoping that one -- or even more -- of those websites will yield a hit.

It is absolutely critical that you have unique passwords for the different websites that you use, and particularly the ones that you use most often. This is especially true for your email accounts, as well as your social media accounts. Since you keep your personal information and confidential data in these accounts, you should take steps to keep these accounts secure. Start with a strong and unique password for each account.

It seems that password leaks are becoming more and more common these days; it seems that we hear about some new instance of account information getting stolen and then leaked to the Internet at large. The only way to protect yourself from these attacks is to use a different password on every site and for every account -- and make sure that you change them frequently. If necessary, use a password manager to help you -- but make sure that this password manager comes from a reliable and trustworthy source!

Use Secure Passwords

Recent password leaks have shown that a lot of people use really simple passwords such as "12345", "letmein" or "iloveyou". This is a risky move and one that can easily be avoided.

Again, using a password manager can be helpful in this case. These managers can help you to come up with secure passwords. Passwords don't necessarily have to be overly long or extremely complicated -- they just have to be strong.

A strong password has a high level of randomness or entropy, which means that it avoids common sequences of letters or numbers. It also doesn't fall easily into patterns that can be inferred from commonplace information such as sequences of numbers that add up to a birthdate or an anniversary, or sequences of letters that resolve into dictionary words.

As I said earlier, I cannot possibly talk about every single security measure that exists under the sun. What most of it boils down to, however, is really nothing more than sheer common sense.

You will need to take the time to make sure that you maintain your security while you use your computer on the Internet.

You will need to make sure that you update your system regularly and that all of your software is up to date. The amount of time that it takes you to do this is nothing compared to the time it will take you to deal with the situation if you do end up a victim of cybercrime, or if you do get hit by a virus or malware attack -- and let's not forget the potential financial costs of such an attack.

Ask yourself this -- is it worth the risk of not taking the time to secure your system? Would you rather be safe or sorry? Or are you prepared to leave it all to chance and hope that, fingers crossed, nothing can or will go wrong?

Think it will never happen to you? Think again!

CONCLUSION

Thank you again for purchasing this book!

I hope this book was able to help you to understand the basics of hacking and penetration testing, as well as the basics of keeping yourself safe while surfing the Internet. For those of you who thought that I would be telling you how to hack into a bank or a major company, sorry to disappoint you. That sort of thing would make me unethical. The best ethical approach I can take is to show you harmless hacking and penetration techniques.

You can go a long way if you want to become an ethical hacker; there are plenty of jobs for those who know exactly what they are doing and big companies that will pay big bucks to make sure their systems are protected. The best place to start is on your own computer system: learn how to protect it and make it secure. It is a great place to learn how a system can be hacked. Once you understand the basics of security then you can go on to learn the basics of hacking and penetration testing.

Take a look around the Internet and you'll find plenty of resources and courses that will teach you how to become an ethical hacker. Once again, I must reiterate that I will not be held responsible for any unethical hacking that arises as a result of the information in this book.

Finally, if you enjoyed this book, then I'd like to ask you for a favor, would you be kind enough to leave a review for this book on Amazon? It'd be greatly appreciated, not just by me but by other potential readers too.

Thank you and good luck!

RESOURCES

Python

Ruby

CSS

JavaScript

PHP

SQL

Reverse Engineering

SecurityFocus Database

MITRE Corporation

PREVIEW OF "LINUX GUIDE FOR BEGINNERS"

LINUX

LINUX GUIDE FOR BEGINNERS: COMMAND LINE, SYSTEM AND OPERATION

CHAPTER 1

THE BASICS

Did you know that due to Android's dominance on smartphones, tablets, and other mobile devices, Linux has turned into one of the largest installed bases in all general-purpose systems?

Although it is not the top pick for desktop computers, Linux remains as an exemplary model of free and open source collaborative projects. Since it operates on embedded systems, it is very useful on television, facility automation controls, video game consoles, network routers, smartwatches, and, as mentioned, mobile devices.

Linux's simplistic design makes it a favorite of programmers. While others like a bit of complexity, some programmers prefer straightforward concepts. In its original nature, it is a leading OS (or Operating System) on mainframe computers, supercomputers, and numerous servers.

As a beginner in Linux, start learning the fundamentals. What are the essentials about Linux?

HISTORY OF LINUX

In 1991, Linux was officially released. Originally, its development centered as a free OS for different Intel x8-based personal computers. Its creator, Linus Torvalds, announced that the OS' creation is partly due to a micro server kernel's unavailability back then.

As an open source collaborative project, its source code is free to use. Under its respective license's term, it can also be modified for commercial and non-commercial distribution.

Since it is compliant with POSIX (or Portable Operating System Interface), Linux is a dependable OS. It has undergone and passed assessment for API (or Application Programming

Interface), standard utility interfaces, and command line shells.

LINUX COMPONENTS

The seamless activities of Linux are attributable to its essential components. There are seven of these.

Seven essential components:

1. Applications availability

   Linux presents the availability of thousands of applications, and these applications are available for immediate installation. It is similar to *Windows Store* and *Apps Store* that lets you search for a preferred application. Once done searching, you can install the app from a centralized location.

2. Daemons

   Daemons are Linux components that serve as background services. Examples of background services are *sound, printing, and scheduling.* These are launched either after a desktop login or during boot.

3. Desktop environments

Desktop environments refer to components with user interaction. Examples are *GNOME, Unity,* and *Cinnamon Enlightenment.* Each of these comes with configuration tools, file managers, calculators, web browsers, and other built-in features.

4. Graphical server

   A graphical server is Linux's subsystem. Its primary duty is displaying graphics on your screen. You can also refer to it as "X" or the "X server".

5. The boot loader

   Linux's management of your computer's boot process is handled by the boot loader. Usually, it is in the form of a splash screen. Once this splash screen pops up, it will slowly proceed into the booting process.

6. The kernel

   Linux's core is called the kernel. It is in charge of management for the memory, peripheral devices, and CPU.

7. The shell

   The shell is Linux's command line. It permits control via typed commands in a text interface.

Made in the USA
Middletown, DE
23 December 2016